VOYAGES

IN ENGLISH

Writing and Grammar

Grade 3 Practice Book

Elaine de Chantal Brookes

Patricia Healey

Irene Kervick

Catherine Irene Masino

Anne B. McGuire

Adrienne Saybolt

3

LOYOLAPRESS.

ISBN-13: 978-0-8294-2104-0; ISBN-10: 0-8294-2104-1

LOYOLAPRESS.
3441 N. ASHLAND AVENUE
CHICAGO, ILLINOIS 60657
(800) 621-1008
www.LoyolaPress.org

08 09 10 11 12 13 14 VH 10 9 8 7 6 5 4 3

CONTENTS

Sentences

● **Add a period after each word group that is a complete sentence. Do not add a period after a word group that is not a sentence. The first one is done for you.**

1. Claire feeds my fish.

2. Beautiful pine trees on the mountains

3. Oscar draws in art class

4. We sat in the shade

5. The green grass

6. Chicago is a large city

7. Liu's cat hid under the bed

8. A bird is sitting on the sign

9. Is next door to my house

10. The bunny ran away

11. Are carrots, potatoes, and peas

12. Randy likes to play tennis

● **Now write the first letter of each complete sentence, in order, on the lines below. If your answers are correct, you will reveal the answer to the riddle.**

What should you use to count cows?

Answer:

A __ C __ __ __ __ - __ __ U __ __ __ __ __ O __

CHAPTER 1

Statements and Questions

● Add periods at the end of statements, or telling sentences. Add question marks at the end of questions, or asking sentences.

1. I went to the zoo with my friend

2. Did you hear the lion roar

3. I ate popcorn and peanuts

4. The sun was shining

5. Where were the lizards and snakes

6. How many animals did you see

7. Antonio saw a giraffe for the first time

8. We rode the bus home

● Write your own statement and question.

9. Statement: _____

_____

10. Question: _____

_____

CHAPTER 1

What Makes a Good Personal Narrative?

● **Circle the word or phrase that correctly completes each sentence.**

1. A personal narrative is a (make-believe   true) story.

2. The topic of a personal narrative is about the (writer   reader).

3. Personal narratives are always told from the (reader's   writer's) point of view.

4. A signal word used often in personal narratives is (*they   I*).

5. The events in a personal narrative are written (out of order   in order).

6. An example of a time word used in a personal narrative is (*give   then*).

7. A good topic for a personal narrative might be a (camping trip   recipe for soup).

● **Circle the topic in each row that could be used for a personal narrative.**

8. my waterskiing adventure   how to snowboard

9. making bird feeders   our trip to the lake

10. the day I met my best friend   the mountains of North America

Question Words

● **Circle the question word that correctly completes each sentence.**

1. (Who   Where) are the markers I bought?

2. (What   When) will the baseball game begin?

3. (Where   What) did you bring for the picnic?

4. (When   Who) is the man talking to our teacher?

5. (Where   What) should I put my backpack?

● **Write a question that you might ask each person. Start each question with *who, what, when,* or *where.***

6. a police officer

_____

7. your teacher

_____

8. the president of the United States

_____

9. a veterinarian

_____

10. a character from a book

_____

CHAPTER 1

Commands

● **Circle *C* if the sentence is a command, *S* if it is a statement, or *Q* if it is a question.**

1. Listen to your teacher.	C	S	Q
2. Tamika, did you walk the dog?	C	S	Q
3. Take out the garbage, Pat.	C	S	Q
4. I heard thunder yesterday.	C	S	Q
5. Are you ready to go to the library?	C	S	Q
6. Push in the chair, please.	C	S	Q
7. Kwan painted a beautiful picture.	C	S	Q
8. Do you help clean the kitchen?	C	S	Q
9. Pour some milk for the cat.	C	S	Q
10. Show your brother the way home.	C	S	Q

● **Write a command that you might hear at school.**

11. _____

_____

CHAPTER

1

Beginning, Middle, and Ending

● Choose a title for a personal narrative from the box. Fill in the story map below with the names of the people in your narrative. Then write where your story takes place. List at least four events in the order that they happened. Then write a sentence about how your personal narrative ends. For an example of a story map, see page 137.

My First Day of School	The Best Friend in the World
A Game I Like to Play	An Awesome Pet

Setting

People

Problem

Events

Ending

CHAPTER 1

Exclamations

● **Add an exclamation point to each sentence that is an exclamation.**

1. I wanted to see the two giraffes

2. How tall they are

3. Do you see the pandas

4. What a cute cub that is

5. The lions are sleeping in the shade

● **Imagine that a storm is coming. Finish each exclamation with words that show strong emotion. Remember to end each one with an exclamation point. The first one has been done for you.**

6. A big storm _____is coming!_____

7. How strong the wind _____

8. Hurry, it's _____

9. What a loud _____

10. The lightning really _____

● **Take turns reading your exclamations with a classmate. Remember to read them with expression.**

Kinds of Sentences

● Write *statement, question, command,* or *exclamation* to tell about each sentence. Then draw a picture of an animal character who might say each sentence.

1. What lovely stripes I have! _____	4. How strange that people don't want to pet me! _____
2. Hang your backpack on my tusk. _____	5. Would you like to play connect-the-spots on my back? _____
3. I think I will go swing on some trees. _____	6. Can you find my pouch? _____

CHAPTER 1

Strong Verbs

● **Match each verb in Column A with a stronger verb in Column B. Write the letter of the matching verb on the line.**

Column A	Column B
1. _____ hold	a. glide
2. _____ cry	b. sob
3. _____ move	c. clutch
4. _____ fall	d. smash
5. _____ show	e. reveal
6. _____ break	f. tumble

● **Choose three strong verbs from Column B. Use each verb in a sentence.**

7. _____

_____

8. _____

_____

9. _____

_____

CHAPTER
1

Subjects

● **Underline the complete subject in each sentence. Then rewrite the sentence with a new subject. The first one is done for you.**

1. <u>Javier</u> ran around the track.

   The athletes ran around the track.

2. My papers fell into the puddle.

   _____

3. The children went to the museum.

   _____

4. Greg found a dollar on the sidewalk.

   _____

5. The ball flew through the air.

   _____

6. Our class reads the newspaper every day.

   _____

7. Katie bought a new blouse.

   _____

8. The squirrels ran through the yard.

   _____

CHAPTER 1

Predicates

● **Underline the complete predicate in each sentence. The first one is done for you.**

1. Ryan <u>made pizza after school</u>.

2. The bird escaped from its cage.

3. Rashad and Trey raced to the top of the hill.

4. Dad cooked dinner last night.

5. The art teacher used pine cones for the bird feeders.

6. My cousin reads all the time.

7. I yanked on the bell cord.

● **Now write the first letter of the first word in each complete predicate, in order, on the numbered lines below. If your answers are correct, you will find the name of the planet that travels the fastest around the sun.**

<u> M </u> <u>   </u> <u>   </u> <u>   </u> <u>   </u> <u>   </u> <u>   </u> travels the fastest around
  1   2   3   4   5   6   7   the sun.

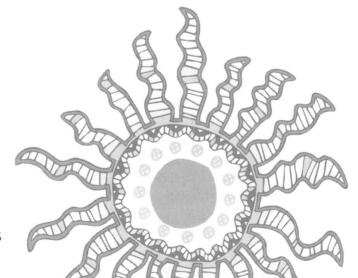

CHAPTER 1

Colorful Adjectives

● **Use adjectives from the word box to complete the sentences.**
Then draw a picture that illustrates each sentence.

crooked	colorful	tiny	curious
odd	terrified	eager	enormous
silly	fearless	attractive	frightened
delighted	lazy	oak	squirming
powerful	famous	ancient	miserable
cheerful	youthful	patient	

The _____ children examined the _____, _____ creature.	Watch how the _____, _____ trainer plays with the _____ gorilla.

Combining Subjects and Predicates

● Complete each pair of sentences with your own subjects or predicates. Then combine the subjects or predicates to make one sentence. The first one is done for you.

1. The dentist <u>cleaned my teeth</u>. The dentist <u>filled a cavity</u>.

   <u>The dentist cleaned my teeth and filled a cavity.</u>

2. Our coach _____. Our coach _____.

   _____

3. _____ went camping. _____ went camping.

   _____

4. _____ planted carrots in the garden. _____ planted carrots in the garden.

   _____

5. My teacher _____. My teacher _____.

   _____

6. The principal _____. The principal _____.

   _____

7. _____ went shopping. _____ went shopping.

   _____

8. The police officer _____. The police officer _____.

   _____

CHAPTER 1

Combining Sentences

● **Combine each pair of sentences. Use the word in parentheses. Write each new sentence. Remember to add a comma before *and* or *but*.**

1. Jay tossed the salad. Megan set the table. (and)

   _____

2. My older brother can drive. I must take the bus. (but)

   _____

3. My friends brought the food. I brought the games. (and)

   _____

4. The movie started on time. We were late. (but)

   _____

5. Paul raked the leaves. Ethan jumped in them. (and)

   _____

6. My mother is a pilot. I hate heights. (but)

   _____

7. James brought the marshmallows. He forgot the graham crackers. (but)

   _____

8. Maria made a snowman. Her brother named it Mr. Shivers. (and)

   _____

CHAPTER 1

Dictionary

● **Find each word listed below in a dictionary. Remember to think about whether the word can be found at the beginning, middle, or end of the dictionary. Then write the page number and guide words for each entry word. The first one is done for you.**

	Page	Guide Words
1. fiesta	263	fiery-figure
2. atlas		
3. pyramid		
4. landscape		
5. reptile		
6. nostril		
7. wampum		
8. gazelle		

CHAPTER 1

Avoiding Run-On Sentences

● **Circle the letter in front of the run-on sentence in each set.**

1. W. I brought the gift, and Mom wrapped it.
   X. The puppies are playing, and the kittens are eating.
   Y. Claire writes poems she does not write stories.

2. M. My best friend moved, but we still call each other.
   O. Ty has a hat, it is brown.
   P. We ordered pizza, and Nick ate three slices.

3. U. Kara writes music, she plays piano.
   V. The telephone rang, and Isabella answered it.
   W. Hannah sang, and Jerrod played the guitar.

4. R. We will see the play, it is in the auditorium.
   S. They went to the library, but it was closed.
   T. I have the towels, and Dad has the sunscreen.

5. L. A squirrel ran up the tree, and it ate an acorn.
   M. Mark cut the lawn, and Kyle trimmed the grass.
   N. The team went on the field, the crowd cheered.

6. A. Brooke found a wallet, she told her teacher.
   B. My hair is curly, and I wear it tied back.
   C. The baby yawned, and he rubbed his eyes.

7. K. Our parakeet chirps, but it never sings.
   L. We ate cookies, and we drank hot cocoa.
   M. Matt entered a contest, he sang a song.

8. D. I drew the pictures, and Ebony wrote the story.
   E. We heard a loud noise, Mom shut the window.
   F. Kate heard the good news, and she jumped for joy.

● **Now write the circled letters, in order, on the numbered lines below. If your answers are correct, you will reveal the answer to the riddle.**

What do you own that is used more often by others?

Answer: ____ ____ ____ ____   ____ ____ ____ ____
            1   2   3   4   5   6   7   8

CHAPTER 1

Self-Assessment

● **Check *Always, Sometimes,* or *Never* to respond to each statement.**

Writing	Always	Sometimes	Never
I can tell about a personal narrative and its features.			
I understand how to write an effective beginning, middle, and end for a personal narrative.			
I can find and use strong verbs.			
I can find and use colorful adjectives.			
I understand how to find a word in a dictionary.			

Grammar	Always	Sometimes	Never
I can name sentences.			
I can name and use statements and questions.			
I can find and use question words.			
I can name and use commands.			
I can name and use exclamations.			
I can name and use the four kinds of sentences.			
I can find and use subjects.			
I can find and use predicates.			
I can combine subjects and predicates to make sentences.			
I can combine two short sentences to form a longer sentence.			
I can name and avoid run-on sentences.			

● **Write the most important thing you learned in this chapter.**

_____

_____

CHAPTER 2

Nouns

● **Underline the two nouns in each sentence.**

1. The grass in the park turned brown.

2. My mother went to the store.

3. Their family lives on a farm.

4. Put the pot in the kitchen.

5. Pineapples grow on that island.

6. Did the boys visit Mexico?

● **In the sentences above six nouns name places. Find and circle these nouns in the word search below.**

```
S  T  O  R  E  B  O  Y  S
E  P  I  S  L  A  N  D  G
F  A  R  M  P  O  T  Y  O
O  R  M  E  X  I  C  O  C
N  K  I  T  C  H  E  N  D
```

CHAPTER 2 Common Nouns and Proper Nouns

● Write each noun in the word box under the correct heading below: *Common Nouns* or *Proper Nouns*.

New York	swing	Cinderella	Taft Elementary School
France	elephant	Nile River	peanut
Uncle Matt	boomerang	towel	singer

Common Nouns   **Proper Nouns**

_____   _____

_____   _____

_____   _____

_____   _____

_____   _____

What Makes a Good How-to Article?

● **Write *yes* if the statement is true or *no* if it is not true.**

1. A how-to article tells how to do something.   _____

2. You should pick a topic that you know nothing about.   _____

3. You should be able to explain the topic in a few short steps.   _____

4. Pick a topic that interests you, but not anyone else.   _____

5. Giving directions to a place might be a good how-to topic.   _____

6. Telling the history of California is a good how-to topic.   _____

7. How-to steps can be listed in any order.   _____

8. It might be a good idea to number the steps in a
   how-to article.   _____

● **Think of a how-to topic that you could explain to a friend. Write it down. Compare your topic with a classmate's topic.**

I would be good at explaining how to _____.

_____

_____

_____

CHAPTER

2 Singular Nouns and Plural Nouns

● **Write the plural form of each noun.**

1. house _____

2. ladder _____

3. hammer _____

4. glass _____

5. lunch _____

6. fox _____

7. ash _____

8. tent _____

9. peach _____

10. pumpkin _____

● **Choose a noun from above. In the boxes below draw a picture that shows it as a singular noun and as a plural noun. Label each picture.**

Singular

_____

Plural

_____

CHAPTER 2

More Plural Nouns

● **Read the paragraph. Then write the plural form of each noun in italics on the lines below.**

Last week children from several *city* (1) spent two *day* (2) on a farm. They rode around the farm in *cart* (3) pulled by *donkey* (4). One group saw rows of trees filled with *cherry* (5). Another group picked *berry* (6) they found on *bush* (7). The farmer also let the children pick *daisy* (8) to take home to their *family* (9). They even played with *bunny* (10) and *puppy* (11). When the children got home, they wrote *story* (12) about their visit.

1. _____

2. _____

3. _____

4. _____

5. _____

6. _____

7. _____

8. _____

9. _____

10. _____

11. _____

12. _____

CHAPTER 2

Parts of a How-to Article

● Choose a how-to topic from the box, or use one of your own. Fill in the sequence chart with your topic idea, a list of steps, and a sentence that tells your conclusion. Remember to list your steps in order. For an example of a sequence chart, see page 137.

how to make a collage	how to dribble a soccer ball
directions to your favorite restaurant	how to play a video game

1.

2.

3.

4.

5.

6.

CHAPTER 2

Irregular Plural Nouns

● **Write the plural form of the noun in parentheses to complete each sentence.**

1. The _____ want to buy the boat. (man)

2. We watched the _____ swim in the pond. (goose)

3. The farmers used _____ to pull carts. (ox)

4. These _____ are waiting for the cashier. (woman)

5. Her _____ are all girls. (child)

6. His _____ are too big for these shoes. (foot)

7. Five _____ are standing near the barn. (sheep)

8. A family of _____ lives in the attic. (mouse)

9. Remember to brush your _____ every day. (tooth)

10. The _____ are walking through the meadow. (deer)

CHAPTER 2
Singular Possessive Nouns

● **Write the singular possessive form of the noun in parentheses to complete each sentence.**

1. I visited _____ house. (Taylor)

2. The _____ backpack is new. (student)

3. _____ story was very funny. (Alma)

4. My _____ tail is orange and white. (cat)

5. Our _____ mascot is a mustang. (school)

● **For each sentence write the name of someone you know on the line. Then rewrite the sentence to show possession. The first one is done for you.**

6. The bicycle belongs to _____Megan_____.

   It is Megan's bicycle._____

7. _____ received a basketball for his birthday.

   _____

8. _____ has a pet iguana.

   _____

9. _____ won an award.

   _____

10. _____ has a new computer.

   _____

CHAPTER
2

Dictionary Meanings

● **Look up each word in a dictionary. Write two meanings for each word. Then write a sentence that shows one meaning of each word.**

1. bob

Meaning 1: _____

Meaning 2: _____

Sentence: _____

2. chorus

Meaning 1: _____

Meaning 2: _____

Sentence: _____

3. stage

Meaning 1: _____

Meaning 2: _____

Sentence: _____

4. jolt

Meaning 1: _____

Meaning 2: _____

Sentence: _____

● **Exchange papers with a classmate. Read each sentence your partner wrote. Tell which meaning of the word is being used.**

CHAPTER 2 Plural Possessive Nouns

● **Write the plural possessive form of the noun in parentheses to complete each sentence.**

1. The _____ trunks are very long. (elephant)

2. The two _____ dresses are pretty. (girl)

3. Those _____ meals were tasty. (chef)

4. All the _____ boots were covered with snow. (caroler)

5. The baby _____ heads bobbed up and down in the water. (swan)

6. The _____ bikes are in the garage. (boy)

7. All of the _____ tests have been graded. (student)

8. The _____ uniforms need to be washed. (player)

9. My _____ rooms are both very messy. (brother)

10. Our _____ home is by a lake. (grandparent)

CHAPTER
2

Irregular Plural Possessive Nouns

● **Write the plural possessive form of each italicized noun.**

1. The *man's* coats are made of leather.   _____

2. The *goose's* feathers feel soft.   _____

3. Are the *child's* toys in the basket?   _____

4. Put the *mouse's* food in that dish.   _____

5. The *woman's* shoes have high heels.   _____

● **Now use each plural possessive noun from above in a sentence of your own.**

6. _____

_____

7. _____

_____

8. _____

_____

9. _____

_____

10. _____

_____

CHAPTER 2

The Four Kinds of Sentences

● Write *statement, question, command,* or *exclamation* to tell about each sentence. There is one of each kind of sentence in each set. Then add the correct punctuation mark at the end of each sentence.

1. a. I will turn on the coffeepot _____

   b. Do you drink coffee _____

   c. Turn on the coffeepot _____

   d. That coffee is very hot _____

2. a. What a great show _____

   b. Did the boys see the lion show _____

   c. Go see the lion show _____

   d. The boys want to see the lion show _____

3. a. Does Kim know how to skateboard _____

   b. What a great skateboard trick _____

   c. Kim knows how to skateboard _____

   d. Show Kim how to skateboard _____

4. a. Put your hat on _____

   b. How cold it is _____

   c. Are you putting on your hat _____

   d. I always wear a hat in winter _____

Collective Nouns

● **Choose four collective nouns from the list below. In each box write a sentence that includes one collective noun and the matching group of animals. An example sentence would be** *The litter of kittens cried all night.* **Then draw a picture for each sentence.**

Collective Nouns: flock (birds), pack (wolves), army (ants), herd (elephants), swarm (bees), litter (kittens)

© Loyola Press

CHAPTER 2

Nouns as Subjects

● **Underline the noun used as the subject in each sentence.**

1. Eduardo looked very excited.

2. The nest is on the lowest branch.

3. Vitamins come in all shapes and colors.

4. The eggs are in the basket.

5. Lisa has to go to soccer practice.

6. The octopus is swimming over the coral.

7. Your pants are in the dryer.

8. Ethan will write his report tonight.

● **Now write the first letter of each subject noun you underlined, in order, on the numbered lines below. If your answers are correct, you will reveal the answer to the riddle.**

What starts with *E*, ends with *E*, and only has one letter in it?

Answer: An _____ _____ _____ _____ _____ _____ _____ _____
                        1   2   3   4   5   6   7   8

CHAPTER

Compound Words

● **Read the letter. Circle the nine compound words.**

Dear Greg,

　　I had the best time visiting your farmhouse. The country is so pretty. Remember the scarecrow we made? Your mom said it would not scare anyone!

　　Watching the beekeeper work at the beehives was fun. I myself would never try that! I did try riding on horseback though. What a great time we had! I liked riding through the fields.

　　The last night was the best! Remember the huge campfire your dad made? I thought we might run out of firewood, but we had enough until bedtime.

　　I hope you can visit me soon. If you do, please bring some of your mom's cornbread!

　　　　　　　　　　　　　　　Your friend,
　　　　　　　　　　　　　　　Casey

● **Now write the two words that make up each compound word you circled on the lines below.**

_____　　_____　　_____

_____　　_____　　_____

_____　　_____　　_____

Words Used as Nouns and Verbs

● Write *noun* or *verb* to tell how the word in italics is used.

1. Will you *ring* the bell? _____

2. That is a pretty *ring* you are wearing. _____

3. Put another *stick* on the fire. _____

4. The glue will *stick* to the cloth. _____

5. Does your dog *bark* all the time? _____

6. We can study the *bark* on the tree. _____

7. John will *blaze* a trail for us. _____

8. The *blaze* was put out by the firefighters. _____

9. Please put the *brush* in the drawer. _____

10. *Brush* your teeth after every meal. _____

11. Kate *files* charts for the doctor. _____

12. Which *files* did you need me to find? _____

Name _____ **Date** _____

Self-Assessment

● Check *Always, Sometimes,* or *Never* to respond to each statement.

Writing	Always	Sometimes	Never
I can tell about a how-to article and its features.			
I include all the parts of a how-to article.			
I understand how to find the meaning of a word in the dictionary.			
I can name and punctuate the four kinds of sentences.			
I can find and write compound words.			

Grammar	Always	Sometimes	Never
I can find and use nouns.			
I can find and use common and proper nouns.			
I can correctly form and use singular and plural nouns.			
I can correctly form and use irregular plural nouns.			
I can correctly form and use singular possessive nouns.			
I can correctly form and use plural possessive nouns.			
I can correctly form and use irregular plural possessive nouns.			
I can find and use collective nouns.			
I can find and use nouns as subjects.			
I can find and use words used as nouns or verbs.			

● **Write the most important thing you learned in this chapter.**

_____

_____

© Loyola Press

34 • Chapter 2 Self-Assessment   Voyages in English 3

CHAPTER 3

Pronouns

● **Underline the personal pronouns in each sentence. Some sentences may have more than one pronoun.**

1. I hope we can go to the zoo tomorrow.

2. She threw it away.

3. Watch them do the latest dance.

4. Do you like apple pie?

5. They are members of the track team.

6. He ate the whole pizza.

● **Be a cartoonist. Draw a funny character on a separate sheet of paper. Write three sentences about the character you drew. Use a pronoun in each sentence.**

7. _____

_____

8. _____

_____

9. _____

_____

CHAPTER 3

Subject Pronouns

● **Underline the subject pronoun in each sentence. Then circle *S* if the pronoun is singular or *P* if it is plural.**

1. They fought over the bone.   S   P

2. It looks good on Leah.   S   P

3. She asked Will to play checkers.   S   P

4. We play catch after school.   S   P

5. Martin, you can jump rope with Justin.   S   P

6. May he come over for dinner?   S   P

7. They rested after their long hike.   S   P

8. It has beautiful trees.   S   P

9. I want to go to the beach.   S   P

10. May we stay up late tonight?   S   P

11. You are the fastest runners.   S   P

12. Later she made popcorn.   S   P

CHAPTER 3

What Makes a Good Description?

● **Circle the letter of the answer that correctly completes each sentence.**

1. A good description _____.
   a. is always funny
   b. leaves the reader with a clear picture of a person, animal, place, or object
   c. explains how to do something

2. Writing a description is like _____ the reader.
   a. painting a picture for
   b. filling out a form for
   c. giving directions to

3. Always choose strong, colorful words that make the readers think about their _____.
   a. audience
   b. paragraph
   c. senses

4. A good thing to do before writing a description is _____.
   a. consider the audience
   b. picture what you are describing in your mind
   c. both *a* and *b*

5. _____ order describes events in the order that they happen.
   a. Time
   b. Space
   c. Open

6. _____ order describes the topic the way that you see it.
   a. Time
   b. Space
   c. Closed

7. Top to _____ is an example of space order.
   a. far
   b. right
   c. bottom

8. *Salty* is a word that appeals to the sense of _____.
   a. smell
   b. touch
   c. taste

9. A word that appeals to the sense of sound is _____.
   a. screeching
   b. chewy
   c. dark

10. *Prickly* is a word that appeals to the sense of _____.
    a. sight
    b. touch
    c. smell

CHAPTER 3

Object Pronouns

● **Underline the personal pronoun in each sentence. Then tell if the pronoun is a subject pronoun or an object pronoun by circling the correct letter.**

1. Bill met him on the corner.
   c. subject pronoun
   d. object pronoun

2. He was standing on his hands.
   o. subject pronoun
   p. object pronoun

3. We could not believe Mr. Fields.
   u. subject pronoun
   v. object pronoun

4. The boys counted them in the harbor.
   f. subject pronoun
   g. object pronoun

5. Lara saw her at the fair.
   g. subject pronoun
   h. object pronoun

6. I hope to go to the beach tomorrow.
   n. subject pronoun
   o. object pronoun

7. The actor took them backstage.
   t. subject pronoun
   u. object pronoun

8. Sue carried it for her neighbor.
   s. subject pronoun
   t. object pronoun

● **Now write the circled letters, in order, on the numbered lines below. If your answers are correct, you will reveal the answer to the riddle.**

What has no beginning, no end, and nothing in the middle?

Answer: A _____ _____ _____ _____ _____ _____ _____ _____
             1   2   3   4   5   6   7   8

CHAPTER 3

Possessive Pronouns

● **Circle the possessive pronoun in each sentence.**

1. Theirs are new.

2. I put mine in the basement.

3. His is silver and shiny.

4. I saw ours at the grocery store.

5. They found theirs in the office.

6. Mine is missing again.

● **Complete the sentence with one of the possessive pronouns you circled above. Then illustrate your sentence in the box.**

7. Your shoes look new. _____ are so grubby.

Writing a Description

● Write sentences to add to the beginning, middle, and ending of the description below. Describe a real place you have visited or make up a place. Remember to use time order or space order in the middle part of your description. Include words that appeal to the reader's senses.

Beginning
I spent time at the most incredible place last summer.

_____

_____

_____

Middle
The thing I remember most about _____ was how it _____.

_____

_____

_____

Ending
_____ is a place I will never forget!

_____

_____

_____

CHAPTER 3

Possessive Adjectives

● **Read the story. Then write a possessive adjective from the word box to complete each sentence. Use each one once. Write your answers on the lines below.**

his	your	Our	our	your
her	my	your	their	

It was Saturday, and David was sitting in _____ room. He could hear his sister, Danielle, in _____ room. They were supposed to be cleaning.

"Did you pick up _____ clothes yet?" asked David.

"No, but I have a plan," said Danielle. "If you help me pick up _____ _____ clothes, I will help you make _____ _____ bed. Then both of _____ rooms will be clean!"

"I like _____ idea!" exclaimed David.

Dale and Danielle cleaned _____ rooms together.

"_____ mother will be very proud of us!" said David.

CHAPTER 3

Agreement of Pronouns and Verbs

● Match each subject pronoun in the first box with a verb from the second box. Write an original sentence using each pair of words. Use the pronoun as the subject. Remember to choose a verb that agrees with the subject pronoun. You may use a verb in more than one sentence.

Subject Pronouns						
I	you	he	she	it	we	they

Verbs						
run	runs	swim	swims	make	makes	read	reads

1. _____

2. _____

3. _____

4. _____

5. _____

6. _____

7. _____

CHAPTER 3

Sensory Words

● Write each sensory word from the word box under the correct heading in the chart. Some words may be written under more than one heading.

clear	silky	flowery	sour	spicy
loud	tapping	tart	slippery	sparkly
round	clattering	minty	smooth	musty
sweet	flat	bumpy	squeaky	pine-scented

See	Hear	Smell	Touch	Taste

● Add your own sensory word to each column. Compare your sensory words with a classmate's words.

CHAPTER 3

I and me

● **Write the pronoun *I* or *me* to complete each sentence correctly.**

1. Dad thanked _____ for my help.

2. _____ earned two dollars.

3. Watch _____ on the trampoline.

4. Yes, _____ washed the dishes.

5. Aunt Elaine invited _____ to the country for a weekend.

6. My sister told _____ about the hiding place.

7. _____ like to skateboard in the park.

8. My friends surprised _____ on my birthday.

● **Write two sentences that tell about an activity you enjoy. Use the pronoun *I* in the first sentence. Use the pronoun *me* in the second sentence.**

9. _____

10. _____

Compound Subjects and Compound Objects

● **Circle the pronouns in these sentences. Then write *compound subject* or *compound object* to tell how the pronouns are used in each sentence.**

1. She and I practiced our speech. _____

2. Sheila invited her and me to the skating party. _____

3. Kiara told us and him. _____

4. You and I are the leaders. _____

5. Keith and they left the practice early. _____

6. The puppies chased Pedro and me. _____

7. He and she worked on their paintings. _____

8. Louise wants Devon and me on the team. _____

9. The teacher picked us and them. _____

10. You and he are the tallest boys. _____

11. They and I are partners. _____

12. Mai asked him and her about the math problem. _____

Five-Senses Chart

● Choose one of the topics below. Then complete the five-senses chart by writing descriptive words or phrases about the topic in each category. For an example of a five-senses chart, see page 140.

Favorite Restaurant	Recess
Birthday Party	Favorite Trip

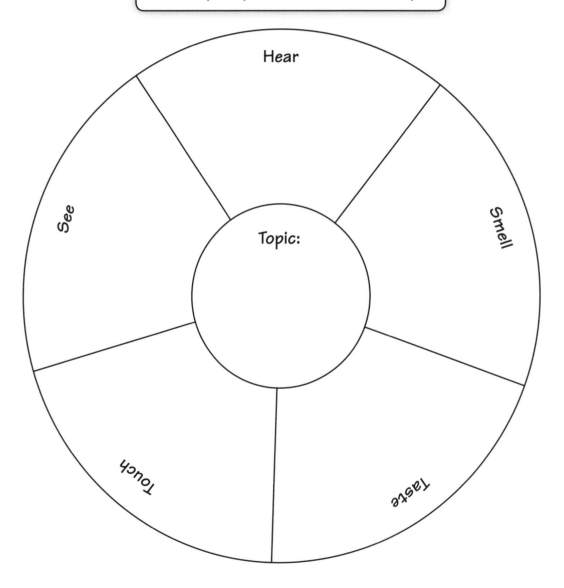

© Loyola Press

CHAPTER 3

Action Verbs

● **Underline the action verb in each sentence.**

1. Owls hoot at night.

2. Her snake slithered around the cage.

3. The rooster crows at daybreak.

4. My frog croaks for food.

5. That mole burrows a new tunnel each day.

6. The kangaroo jumped over the log.

● **Write your own sentences about animals using the action verbs below. Use a singular noun as the subject.**

7. (oinks) _____

_____

8. (flies) _____

_____

9. (swims) _____

_____

10. (roars) _____

_____

CHAPTER

3

Being Verbs

● **Underline the verb in each sentence. Then write *action* or *being* on the line to tell what kind it is.**

1. My family is very large.   _____

2. She was very sick.   _____

3. The dog digs in the garden.   _____

4. The stars are bright tonight.   _____

5. Wanda washed the dishes.   _____

6. His brother drives a car.   _____

● **Circle the being verb that correctly completes each sentence.**

7. My cocoa (were   is) cold.

8. Mike (was   are) late again yesterday.

9. Those cookies (was   are) tasty.

10. Nicole's hamsters (are   am) fluffy.

11. Someday I (will be   have been) a grown-up.

12. We (is   were) ready for the test.

CHAPTER 3

Synonyms

● **Circle the two words in each row that are synonyms.**

1. new   modern   old

2. large   small   huge

3. funny   silly   sad

4. boring   wonderful   marvelous

5. show   cover   hide

6. tidy   neat   sloppy

● **Write the words from above that are not circled on the lines below. Then write a synonym for each word.**

7. _____   _____

8. _____   _____

9. _____   _____

10. _____   _____

11. _____   _____

12. _____   _____

CHAPTER 3

Helping Verbs

● **Circle the correct letter to tell if the italicized verb in each sentence is an action verb, a being verb, or a helping verb.**

1. My friend *plays* the piano.
   h. action verb
   i. being verb
   j. helping verb

2. The cheetah *leaped* into the tree.
   a. action verb
   b. being verb
   c. helping verb

3. Stewart *will* sleep all night long.
   p. action verb
   q. being verb
   r. helping verb

4. This *is* my favorite song.
   d. action verb
   e. being verb
   f. helping verb

5. She *can* see her brother.
   j. action verb
   k. being verb
   l. helping verb

6. Steve *folded* a paper airplane.
   a. action verb
   b. being verb
   c. helping verb

7. We *might* stay for the lecture.
   l. action verb
   m. being verb
   n. helping verb

8. I *am* in the school play!
   d. action verb
   e. being verb
   f. helping verb

● **Now write the circled letters, in order, on the numbered lines below. If your answers are correct, you will reveal the answer to the riddle.**

How do rabbits travel?

Answer: by _____ _____ _____ _____ p _____ _____ _____ _____
          1   2   3   4   5   6   7   8

© Loyola Press

Name _____ **Date** _____

CHAPTER 3

Self-Assessment

● Check *Always*, *Sometimes*, or *Never* to respond to each statement.

Writing	Always	Sometimes	Never
I can tell about a description and its features.			
I understand how to write the beginning, middle, and ending of a description.			
I can name and use sensory words.			
I understand how to use a five senses chart.			
I can find and use synonyms.			

Grammar	Always	Sometimes	Never
I can find and use pronouns.			
I can find and use subject pronouns.			
I can find and use object pronouns.			
I can find and use possessive pronouns.			
I can find and use possessive adjectives.			
I can show correct agreement between a pronoun used as a subject and the verb.			
I understand when to use the pronouns *I* and *me*.			
I can find and use pronouns in compound subjects and objects.			
I can find and use action verbs.			
I can find and use being verbs.			
I can find and use helping verbs.			

● Write the most interesting thing you learned in this chapter.

_____

_____

CHAPTER 4

Principal Parts of Verbs

● Write *present, present participle, past,* or *past participle* to tell the form of the italicized verb in each sentence.

1. Len is *cooking* hot dogs for dinner. _____

2. Dad *chopped* all the firewood. _____

3. Aunt Doris is *working* at the bank. _____

4. The girls have *cleaned* their rooms. _____

5. The worm *crawled* on the leaf. _____

6. The salesclerks *smile* at everyone. _____

● Write the present, present participle, past, and past participle form of each verb from the sentences above. The first one is done for you.

	Present	Present Participle	Past	Past Participle
7.	cook	cooking	cooked	cooked
8.				
9.				
10.				
11.				
12.				

CHAPTER 4
Regular Verbs and Irregular Verbs

● **Write *R* if the italicized verb in each sentence is regular or *IR* if it is irregular.**

1. Cathy *sang* the national anthem at the game. _____

2. Andre and I *painted* the chairs blue. _____

3. The baby bird *flew* out of its nest. _____

4. The doctor *helped* the injured boy. _____

5. I *talked* on the phone for an hour. _____

6. She *gave* the clerk a dollar. _____

7. Our class *wrote* a letter to students in Mexico. _____

● **There are four irregular verbs in the sentences above. Find and circle these verbs in the word search below.**

```
K  P  F  S  A  N  G  E  W
S  A  L  B  N  T  A  C  F
A  I  E  M  A  C  V  L  L
T  O  W  R  O  T  E  W  O
```

CHAPTER 4

What Makes a Good Personal Letter?

● **Name the part of a personal letter described in each statement. Write the letter of the correct part on the line.**

a. heading	c. body	e. signature
b. greeting	d. closing	

1. This part gives the name of the receiver. _____

2. This part is at the bottom above your name. _____

3. This part is the message of the letter. _____

4. This part gives the address of the writer. _____

5. This part can have several paragraphs. _____

6. This part is where you write your full name. _____

7. This part is in the top right-hand corner. _____

8. This part often starts with *Dear*. _____

9. This part has a date. _____

10. This part might have the words *Yours truly*. _____

CHAPTER 4

Bring, Buy, Come, and *Sit*

● **Circle the verb that correctly completes each sentence.**

1. Arturo is (bringing   brought) my glasses.

2. The explorer (bring   brought) food for the long journey.

3. Mr. Patel was (bought   buying) a new toy for the cat.

4. Richard (buy   bought) the movie poster for his dad.

5. Josie has (come   came) to each new play.

6. Michelle's invitation is (came   coming) in the mail.

7. Ms. Black had (sit   sat) down for a while to rest.

8. I am (sitting   sat) with my best friend.

9. Please (bring   brought) your coat with you.

10. We have (buy   bought) fruit from that store before.

● **Four of the sentences above have verbs in the present participle form. Circle the number next to these sentences.**

CHAPTER
4

Eat, Go, and See

● **Write the letter of the verb that correctly completes each sentence.**

1. _____ We have _____ here many times. a. saw

2. _____ They _____ two movies this weekend. b. went

3. _____ I _____ my lunch at noon every day. c. going

4. _____ Mel is _____ to the mall with me. d. eaten

5. _____ The boys _____ to the game last week. e. seen

6. _____ She has _____ the play three times. f. eat

● **Now write _present, present participle, past,_ or _past participle_ to tell the form of the verb used in each sentence above.**

7. Sentence 1: _____

8. Sentence 2: _____

9. Sentence 3: _____

10. Sentence 4: _____

11. Sentence 5: _____

12. Sentence 6: _____

CHAPTER 4

The Body of a Personal Letter

● Imagine that your favorite book or movie character is writing a personal letter. Write a two-paragraph thank-you letter from this character to another character. For example, one pig from *The Three Little Pigs* could thank his brother for saving him from the big bad wolf. Remember to write about one topic at a time.

_____

_____

_____

_____

Dear _____,

_____

_____

_____

_____

_____

_____

_____

_____

_____

_____,

_____

© Loyola Press

CHAPTER 4

Take, Tear, and Write

• **Write the correct form of *take, tear,* or *write* to complete each sentence.**

1. Please _____ some leftovers with you. (take)

2. I was angry because the baby _____ a page from my new book. (tear)

3. Henry has _____ a letter to his uncle. (write)

4. Casey is _____ down the recipe for me. (write)

5. May has _____ holes in the paper to make a mask. (tear)

6. Logan _____ the test last Tuesday. (take)

7. The demolition crew was _____ down the old library. (tear)

8. The principal _____ a note to her secretary yesterday. (write)

9. Nicholas is _____ piano lessons. (take)

10. _____ off that tag before you wear your new shirt. (tear)

11. Chiara has _____ two courses this fall. (take)

12. I _____ an e-mail to my friend every week, and she sends me one back. (write)

Simple Present Tense

● **Circle the verb that correctly completes each sentence.**

1. My parents (makes   make) a garden every year.

2. My mother (love   loves) flowers.

3. She (plant   plants) many different kinds of flowers.

4. They (bloom   blooms) all summer long.

5. My father (grow   grows) wonderful vegetables.

6. His tomatoes (taste   tastes) great.

7. The squirrels sometimes (get   gets) to them first.

8. We (help   helps) in the garden.

● **Write a sentence for each simple present tense verb.**

9. waters

_____

10. rains

_____

11. eat

_____

12 pick

_____

CHAPTER 4

Filling Out Forms

● **Complete this form to enter your best friend in the Best Friend Contest. Your best friend can be a family member, someone else you know, or even a pet. Remember to carefully reread your completed form.**

Name: _____

Address: _____

City: _____ State: _____ Zip Code: _____

Name of your best friend: _____

How long have you known your best friend? _____

Where did you meet him or her? _____

What three words best describe your best friend? _____

_____

Why does he or she deserve this award? _____

_____

_____

_____

Simple Past Tense

● Write the simple past tense of each verb.

1. pay   _____   5. go   _____

2. grow   _____   6. learn _____

3. cheer   _____   7. win   _____

4. shout   _____   8. play   _____

● Write sentences using four of the simple past tense verbs from above.

9. _____

_____

10. _____

_____

11. _____

_____

12. _____

_____

CHAPTER
4

Future Tense with *Will*

● Write two sentences that tell what you think you will do during each of the future times described below. Use the helping verb *will* in each sentence. The first one is done for you.

Future time: Tonight

1. I will eat dinner. _____

2. _____

Future time: Tomorrow

3. _____

4. _____

Future time: This weekend

5. _____

6. _____

Future time: Next summer

7. _____

8. _____

Future time: 20 years from now

9. _____

10. _____

CHAPTER 4

Compound Subjects

● **Choose two nouns and one verb from the lists below. Use these words in a sentence that has a compound subject. Then draw a picture that illustrates your sentence.**

Nouns: Jerry, Kate, tiger, monkey, doctor, firefighter

Verbs: ate, flew, crawled, skated, ran, helped, looked, stayed

Sentence: _____

● **Share your sentence and picture with a classmate. Then together make up a new sentence with a compound subject.**

_____

CHAPTER 4

Future Tense with *Going To*

● **Write two sentences for each verb. Use the future tense with *going to* in the first sentence. Use the simple past tense in the second sentence. The first one is done for you.**

1. push

Future: I am going to push Kara on the swing. _____

Past: I pushed Kara on the swing. _____

2. sing

Future: _____

Past: _____

3. wait

Future: _____

Past: _____

4. play

Future: _____

Past: _____

5. plant

Future: _____

Past: _____

6. drive

Future: _____

Past: _____

Present Progressive Tense

● **Answer each question by writing a sentence with a verb in the present progressive tense.**

1. Carmen is mixing the batter.

   Carmen is pouring it into the round pan.

   Carmen is putting the pan into the oven.

   What is Carmen doing? _____

2. Pepper is running in the yard.

   Dan is throwing a Frisbee.

   Pepper is leaping into the air.

   What is Pepper doing? _____

3. Dan is standing by the microphone.

   The band is playing.

   Dan is opening his mouth.

   What is Dan doing? _____

4. Mary is sitting in a big chair.

   She is looking at a book.

   She is turning pages.

   What is Mary doing? _____

● **Underline the verbs in the present progressive tense in the sentences above.**

CHAPTER 4

Antonyms

● Fill in each mini-word web by writing a synonym and an antonym for the word in the middle. Write an *S* above the synonym and an *A* above the antonym. The first one is done for you. For another example of a word web, see page 139.

       A   S   A   S

1. (happy)—(glum)—(sad)   6. ( )—(brave)—( )

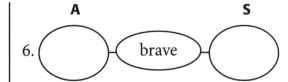

2. ( )—(hot)—( )   7. ( )—(fast)—( )

3. ( )—(pretty)—( )   8. ( )—(bad)—( )

4. ( )—(shut)—( )   9. ( )—(bumpy)—( )

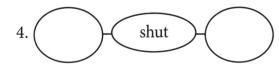

5. ( )—(bent)—( )   10. ( )—(bright)—( )

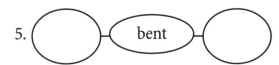

CHAPTER 4

Past Progressive Tense

● Imagine that you went on a terrible camping trip and wrote the following letter to a friend. Complete the letter. Write the past progressive tense of a verb from the word box on each line. Use each verb only once.

blow	chirp	doze	fall
howl	rain	sneeze	

_____
_____
_____
_____
(inside address and date)

Dear _____,
(your friend's name)

    Last weekend my family went on the worst camping trip ever!

The weather was terrible. It (1) _____ most of the time.

It (2) _____ when we arrived. Our clothes got all wet.

The wind (3) _____ hard when we tried to put up our tent.

That was bad. But the worst part was trying to get to sleep. Just as I

(4) _____ off, several coyotes started to howl. They

(5) _____ most of the night. Then in the morning

the birds (6) _____ . By Sunday, we were all sick. We

(7) _____ all day!

    I hope that you had a better weekend than I did.

                        Your friend,

                        _____

CHAPTER
4

Self-Assessment

● Check *Always, Sometimes,* or *Never* to respond to each statement.

Writing	Always	Sometimes	Never
I can tell about the features of a personal letter.			
I understand the purpose of a personal letter and how to organize the body of it.			
I can correctly fill out a form.			
I can find and use compound subjects.			
I can find and use antonyms.			

Grammar	Always	Sometimes	Never
I can find and form the principal parts of verbs.			
I can find and form regular and irregular verbs.			
I can find and form the irregular verbs *bring, buy, come,* and *sit*.			
I can find and form the irregular verbs *eat, go,* and *see*.			
I can find and form the irregular verbs *take, tear,* and *write*.			
I can find and use verbs in the simple present tense.			
I can find and use verbs in the simple past tense.			
I can find and use verbs in the future tense with *will*.			
I can find and use verbs in the future tense with *going to*.			
I can find and use verbs in the present progressive tense.			
I can find and use verbs in the past progressive tense.			

● Write the most meaningful thing you learned in this chapter.

_____

CHAPTER 5

Is and Are, Was and Were

● **Circle the verb that correctly completes each sentence.**

1. The dog (is   are) digging in the yard.

2. The babies (is   are) in the nursery.

3. My cats (was   were) on the bed.

4. The seals (was   were) in the ocean.

5. Mom (is   are) at her office.

6. The apples (is   are) ready to be picked from the orchard.

7. A ball (is   are) rolling across the grass.

● **Four sentences from above have plural subjects. Find and circle these plural subjects in the word search below.**

P	B	Y	A	C	A	T	S	J	K
A	N	E	B	A	B	I	E	S	S
I	Y	S	T	M	O	N	A	P	K
P	U	L	R	I	W	S	L	G	B
C	I	A	P	P	L	E	S	U	T

CHAPTER
5

Contractions
with *Not*

● **Write a contraction for the italicized word or words in each sentence.**

1. Kelly *was not* going to make the flight.   _____

2. They *are not* staying up late tonight.   _____

3. Tom *did not* finish his homework.   _____

4. I *will not* be able to attend the party.   _____

5. Mr. Pell *cannot* carry the paint cans for you.   _____

6. My homework *is not* in my backpack.   _____

7. She *does not* need to make up that quiz.   _____

8. Mary *is not* able to visit her aunt.   _____

9. We *do not* have time to clean our rooms.   _____

10. The boys *were not* running in the hall.   _____

● **Write a sentence of your own using one of the contractions from above.**

11. _____

_____

CHAPTER 5

What Makes a Good Book Report?

● Write *beginning, middle,* or *end* to tell which part of a book report each statement describes.

1. Write the complete title. _____

2. Tell what you think about the book. _____

3. Spell the author's name correctly. _____

4. Tell what the story is about. _____

5. Introduce the characters. _____

6. Don't tell too much about the ending. _____

7. Describe the setting. _____

8. Tell which parts of the book you liked. _____

9. Describe the important events in the story. _____

10. Give reasons for your opinion about the book. _____

CHAPTER 5 Identifying Adjectives

● **Underline the adjective in each sentence. Circle the noun it describes.**

1. Peter, please help me lift the heavy box.

2. The loud music made me want to dance.

3. I need a warm blanket.

4. Nick wore a spooky costume to the party.

5. Mrs. Hunter took us to see the newborn puppies.

6. Sarah and Robert watch scary movies on TV.

● **For each sentence above write a new adjective on the lines below.**

7. _____

8. _____

9. _____

10. _____

11. _____

12. _____

CHAPTER 5

Adjectives Before Nouns

● The time is 50 years from now. You have been chosen to design a uniform for the students at your school. Draw a picture of the uniform. Write at least three sentences that describe the uniform. Include adjectives before the nouns in your sentences. Underline each adjective.

_____

_____

_____

CHAPTER 5 Character and Plot

● Use the idea web to help you organize information for a book report. Write the title of a book you have read in the center circle. Then write words and phrases to complete each side circle. For an example of an idea web, see page 139.

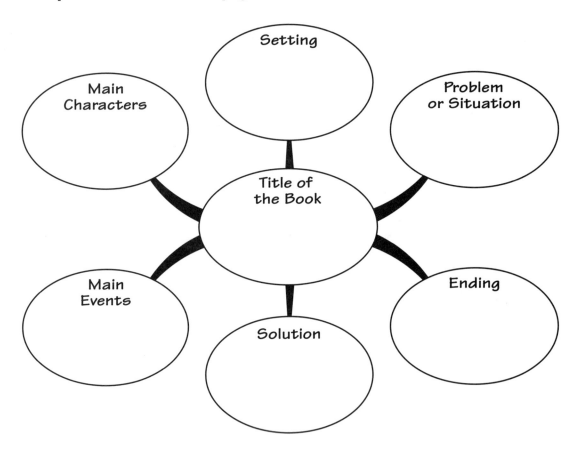

Subject Complements

CHAPTER 5

● **Underline the adjective used as a subject complement in each sentence.**

1 The spring carnival is exciting.

2. The roller coaster ride was scary.

3. These treats are tasty.

4. The line for the Ferris wheel is long.

5. Those games were hard.

6. After a day at the carnival my feet were sore.

● **Picture an outdoor place you have seen or visited. Describe this place by completing each sentence with an adjective used as a subject complement. Choose adjectives from the word box or use your own.**

peaceful	beautiful	blue	gold	tall	colorful
majestic	calm	sunny	cold	huge	delicious
grand	noisy	green	awesome		

7. The sky is _____.

8. The weather is _____.

9. The trees are _____.

10. The leaves are _____.

11. All of the flowers are _____.

12. This place is _____.

CHAPTER 5

Compound Subject Complements

● Underline the adjectives used as subject complements in each sentence. Circle the letter at the end of the sentence if the sentence has a compound subject complement.

1. The berries we picked were red and sweet.   V

2. Dan's book is good.   J

3. The candles on the table are tall and bright.   I

4. The game I watched was long.   A

5. Those fish we saw were pretty.   P

6. Jesse's collection is interesting and unique.   R

7. The bus Josh and Kathy took was slow and late.   U

8. That box by the door is heavy.   E

9. Mom's cake was delicious.   R

10. The watch he lost was old and valuable.   S

● Now write the circled letters, in order, on the lines below. If your answers are correct, you will reveal the answer to the riddle.

Why did the computer go to the doctor?

Answer: It had a _____ _____ _____ _____ _____!

CHAPTER 5

Parts of a Book

● **Write the part of a book that answers each riddle.**

1. What's my title?
   Who published this book?
   It's printed on my page.
   Just take a look!

   _____

2. Order. Order.
   Alphabetical please.
   Find all of your topics
   Here with ease.

   _____

3. What does that word mean?
   Do you know?
   I have its definition in ABC order.
   So here you should go!

   _____

4. You want to know
   Where you can read about cucumbers.
   On my page you'll find the chapter
   And the beginning page number.

   _____

5. You have one of these
   Down the middle of your back.
   I have one, too.
   Just pull me from the stack.

   _____

● **Now write your own riddle about the cover of a book on the lines
below. Then share your riddle with a partner.**

_____

_____

_____

_____

Adjectives That Compare

● **Circle the adjective that correctly completes each sentence. Then write 2 on the line if the sentence compares two things. Write *more than 2* if the sentence compares more than two things.**

1. My gerbil is (bigger   biggest) than Sue's.   _____

2. Larry's pumpkin is the (smaller   smallest) of all.   _____

3. Her pillow is the (fluffier   fluffiest) of the four.   _____

4. Is that dog the (larger   largest) in town?   _____

5. Of the two suitcases Sam's is (heavier   heaviest).   _____

6. My sandcastle is (taller   tallest) than Jody's.   _____

7. A boa constrictor is (longer   longest) than a rattlesnake.   _____

8. This elephant is the (bigger   biggest) animal in the zoo.   _____

9. This movie was the (funnier   funniest) one I've ever seen.   _____

10. My sister is (older   oldest) than my brother.   _____

CHAPTER 5

Irregular Adjectives That Compare

● **Use the adjectives *good, better,* and *best* to complete the story.**

Colleen was a (1) _____ sport at the soccer game today.

She knew she was a (2) _____ player than Nicole. In fact, everyone

thought Colleen was the (3) _____ player on the team. But Nicole's

grandmother was visiting from out of town. Nicole would not play unless

Colleen got hurt. Colleen wanted to be a (4) _____ friend, so

she told the coach to let Nicole play for her today. Colleen thought this was

a (5) _____ idea than Nicole did. However, Nicole changed her

mind when she played the (6) _____ game of her life!

● **Use the adjectives *bad, worse,* and *worst* to complete the story.**

Today was the (7) _____ day of the week! I knew it was

going to be a (8) _____ day when my alarm clock did not

ring. The weather was (9) _____ today than yesterday. I got a

(10) _____ grade on my math homework. I dropped my lunch

in a puddle, and later, my dentist gave me the (11) _____ news

of the week. I have two cavities! This visit was (12) _____ than

my last one. When my mom saw me at home, she just smiled and gave me

a hug. She told me to look at the bright side. Tomorrow cannot be any

(13) _____ than today!

CHAPTER
5

Compound Predicates

● **Underline the compound predicate in each sentence.**

1. The outfielder leaped into the air and caught the fly ball.

2. On the weekends I roller-skate and ride my bike.

3. Our teacher stood in front of the class and read the story.

4. The leaves fell from the tree and blew across the lawn.

5. My brother plays the guitar and sings in a band.

6. The ball bounced over the fence and rolled into the street.

● **Draw a picture that illustrates one of the sentences from above. Share your picture with a partner. Then together make up a new sentence with a compound predicate.**

7. Our new sentence: _____

_____

Name _____ Date _____

Adjectives That Tell How Many

● Underline the adjective that tells how many about the italicized noun in each sentence. Then circle the letter under *A* if the adjective tells about how many or the letter under *E* if it tells exactly how many.

	A	E
1. There are many *cars* in the parking lot.	T	A
2. You'll need three *cups* of flour.	B	H
3. I'll take a dozen *bagels*.	K	E
4. A few *birds* flew into the tree.	L	J
5. Several *students* were absent.	E	A
6. I am feeding some *cats*.	T	E
7. Kyle brought two *cans* of corn.	R	T
8. Marina is looking at a few *courses*.	E	B
9. Many *people* chose that class.	R	O
10. Kari sits in the fifth *seat*.	R	G

● Now write the circled letters, in order, on the numbered lines below. If your answers are correct, you will reveal the answer to the riddle.

What always ends everything?

Answer: ____ ____ ____ ____ ____ ____ ____ ____ ____ ____ !
       1   2   3   4   5   6   7   8   9   10

CHAPTER 5

Articles

● **Underline the sentence in each pair in which the article is used correctly. In the other sentence cross out the article that is used incorrectly and write the correct article. The first one is done for you.**

1. <u>I have never been to a zoo.</u>

   I have never been to ~~a~~ ^{an} airport.

2. My mother lost an umbrella.

   My mother lost a earring.

3. An ant walked across the picnic table.

   An fly walked across the picnic table.

4. An icicle hung from the roof.

   An flag hung from the roof.

5. There was a orange on the floor.

   There was a pea on the floor.

6. She has an letter in her hand.

   She has an envelope in her hand.

CHAPTER 5

Prefixes

● **Match each word from the word box with its definition. Write the letters of the word in the blanks.**

uncertain	repaint	unsafe	uneven
unclear	uncooked	relive	refold

1. to paint again ____ ____ ____ ____ ____ ____
    4

2. to fold again ____ ____ ____ ____ ____ ____
    1

3. to live again ____ ____ ____ ____ ____ ____
    2

4. not certain ____ ____ ____ ____ ____ ____ ____ ____ ____
    6

5. not cooked ____ ____ ____ ____ ____ ____ ____ ____
    5

6. not safe ____ ____ ____ ____ ____ ____
    8

7. not even ____ ____ ____ ____ ____ ____
    7

8. not clear ____ ____ ____ ____ ____ ____ ____
    3

● **Now write the numbered letters on the matching numbered lines below. If your answers are correct, you will reveal the answer to the riddle.**

What do birds use for napkins?

Answer: ____ ____ ____ ____ ____ ____ ____ ____
           1   2   3   4   5   6   7   8

Demonstrative Adjectives

● **Circle the sentence with the correct demonstrative adjective to answer each question.**

1. Which painting is *closer*?

   We bought this painting at the art fair.

   My friend gave me that painting.

2. Which bicycle is *closer*?

   That bicycle is the one I want.

   This bicycle is mine.

3. Which bookcase is *farther* away?

   That bookcase has three shelves.

   This bookcase has five shelves.

4. Which toy is *farther* away?

   This toy is by the dog.

   That toy belongs to the baby.

5. Which car is *closer*?

   My dad is thinking of buying this car.

   We loaded our suitcases into that car.

● **Write two sentences that include a demonstrative adjective. Write about a thing that is near in the first sentence and about a thing that is far away in the second sentence.**

6. _____

7. _____

CHAPTER 5

Self-Assessment

● Check *Always, Sometimes,* or *Never* to respond to each statement.

Writing	Always	Sometimes	Never
I can tell about the features of a book report.			
I understand how to describe the characters and plot in a book report.			
I can name and use the different parts of a book.			
I can find and use compound predicates.			
I can find the prefixes *un-* and *re-* and use them to understand the meanings of words.			

Grammar	Always	Sometimes	Never
I understand when to use the verbs *is, are* and *was, were.*			
I can find and form contractions with *not.*			
I can find and use adjectives.			
I can find and use adjectives before nouns.			
I can find and use subject complements.			
I can find and use compound subject complements.			
I can find and use adjectives that compare.			
I can find and use irregular adjectives that compare.			
I can find and use adjectives that tell how many.			
I can find and use articles.			
I can find and use demonstrative adjectives.			

● **Write the most practical thing you learned in this chapter.**

_____

_____

CHAPTER 6

Proper Adjectives

● **Write a *P* above the proper adjective in each sentence. Then rewrite each sentence using a capital letter for the proper adjective.**

1. For dinner we ate spicy texan chili.

   _____

2. Mother received lovely english china from her grandmother.

   _____

3. Did you see the mysterious egyptian writing on the pyramid?

   _____

4. The skirt was made from colorful indian cloth.

   _____

5. The energetic girls performed an irish dance for us.

   _____

6. The american scientist worked tirelessly on the complex project.

   _____

7. We are going to celebrate at a small japanese restaurant.

   _____

8. The whole family lives only miles from the canadian border.

   _____

Name _____ **Date** _____

CHAPTER 6

Nouns Used as Adjectives

● **Match the nouns to make eight phrases. Use the nouns in the first column as adjectives before the nouns in the second column. Write the word from the second column on the line. The first one is done for you.**

1. cowboy	_____ hat _____	a. food
2. baseball	_____	b. garden
3. porch	_____	~~c. hat~~
4. snack	_____	d. finger
5. ring	_____	e. café
6. rose	_____	f. field
7. insect	_____	g. light
8. sidewalk	_____	h. bite

● **Write sentences using two of the phrases from above.**

9. _____

_____

10. _____

_____

CHAPTER 6

What Makes Good Persuasive Writing?

● **Use a word from the word box to complete each sentence. Write the word on the line. You will not use all of the words in the word box.**

topic	reasons	how-to	three	questions
audience	persuasive	research	two	believe

1. A letter to the editor is an example of _____ writing.

2. In a persuasive article, the reasons you give should interest your

   _____ .

3. The _____ is what you want your audience to believe or do.

4. Interviewing people and searching the Internet are examples of

   doing _____ .

5. Explanations that defend the way you feel are sometimes called

   _____ .

6. Give at least _____ reasons that support your topic in a persuasive article.

7. Persuasive writing asks people to _____ or do something.

CHAPTER 6

Adverbs

● **Underline the adverb in each sentence.**

1. Let's walk slowly through the garden.

2. Today I'm going to finish my homework.

3. Jorge put the cat inside for the night.

4. Handle the eggs carefully.

5. Someone is practicing the trumpet nearby.

6. Luisa has not been to the planetarium before.

7. Albert always takes a lunch to school.

8. Steve walked hurriedly to the fire exit.

9. Ann went outside to eat her sandwich.

● **Write each adverb from above under the question that it answers.**

When?	Where?	How?
_____	_____	_____
_____	_____	_____
_____	_____	_____

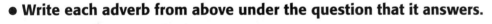

CHAPTER 6 Adverbs That Tell *When* or *How Often*

● **Underline the adverb that tells *when* or *how often* in each sentence.**

1. He has not gone yet.

2. The girls arrived at the party early.

3. I sometimes ride my bike to my friend's house.

4. Then the bird flew to its nest.

5. Eventually I will be able to hit that high note.

6. The jogger exercises regularly.

7. The newspaper arrives at our house daily.

8. Adam hurt his ankle again.

9. Mr. Drake visits his doctor yearly.

● **Now write the first letter of each adverb you underlined, in order, on the numbered lines below. If your answers are correct, the letters will spell an adverb that tells *when*.**

___ ___ ___ ___ ___ ___ ___ ___ ___
 1   2   3   4   5   6   7   8   9

Beginning, Middle, and Ending

● Read the persuasive article. Circle the topic sentence. Underline the two reasons the writer uses to persuade the reader. Draw a box around the sentence that retells the topic.

It is 3:30 p.m., and I am walking up the steps to my family's apartment. I start to smile when I hear the sounds of crying and footsteps on the other side of our door. I know there is someone special to greet me every day. He is my dog, Louie. I think that dogs make the best pets.

Dogs make great playmates. You always have a friend around if you own a dog. Louie is playful and full of energy. My mom likes it when I play with Louie because it keeps me busy and active.

Dogs can also learn to do tricks. Teaching Louie how to roll over has taught me many things. It has shown me how being patient and not giving up can be rewarded. It has also shown me that dogs are smart.

As a dog owner, I have many responsibilities. Feeding Louie and walking him are jobs I must do every day. But I don't mind. I am lucky to have the greatest pet in the world—a dog!

CHAPTER 6

Adverbs That Tell *Where*

● **Underline the adverb that tells *where* in each sentence.**

1. Dad moved the furniture inside.

2. The boat moved forward in the water.

3. Who let the dogs in?

4. Pedro came downstairs to study.

5. The hawk flew high over the land.

6. Mai is going away for the weekend.

7. Please put your jackets here.

8. We watched as the ducks swam nearby.

9. The hikers traveled far to reach the mountaintop.

10. I have looked everywhere for my backpack.

● **Write a sentence with one of the adverbs in the word box.**
Draw a picture of your sentence.

| backward | forward | inside | outside |

CHAPTER 6

Adverbs That Tell *How*

● **Underline the adverb that tells *how* in each sentence.**

1. The popcorn popped loudly.

2. Patty carefully signed her name.

3. Mike slowly ate his dinner.

4. Both students walked proudly home.

5. I will bathe the puppy gently.

6. The elephant stormed noisily through the jungle.

7. The geese swam quickly across the pond.

8. We must talk quietly about the surprise party.

9. He waited sadly by the steps.

10. The player swung clumsily at the ball.

● **Write a sentence of your own with one of the adverbs above.
Draw a picture of your sentence.**

_____

_____

CHAPTER 6 Idea Webs

● Complete the idea web with information about a persuasive topic you would like to write about. Choose a topic from the box or a topic of your own. Remember to include your topic, reasons, and ideas that support your reasons. Add more lines and circles if necessary. For an example of an idea web see page 139.

> It would be fun to be a twin.
>
> Our school needs to have more recess time during the day.
>
> All children should be allowed to have a pet.
>
> Our city should offer more sports and recreation classes.

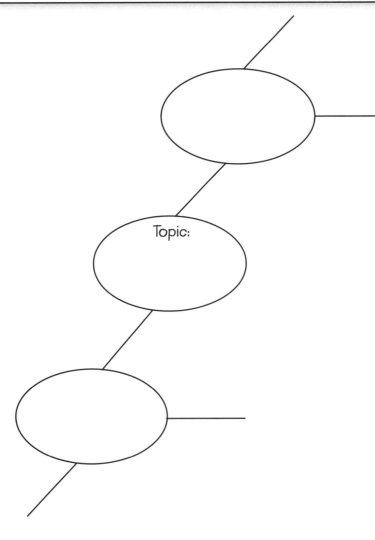

© Loyola Press

CHAPTER

6

Negatives

● **Change each sentence to express a negative idea in three different ways. Follow the directions in parentheses. The first set of sentences is done for you.**

1. It is snowing.

    a. It is not snowing. _____ (Add *not*.)

    b. It isn't snowing. _____ (Make a contraction.)

    c. It never snows. _____ (Add *never*.)

2. You are competing.

    a. _____ (Add *not*.)

    b. _____ (Make a contraction.)

    c. _____ (Add *never*.)

3. I am working.

    a. _____ (Add *not*.)

    b. _____ (Make a contraction.)

    c. _____ (Add *never*.)

4. The dog was barking.

    a. _____ (Add *not*.)

    b. _____ (Make a contraction.)

    c. _____ (Add *never*.)

● **Rewrite each sentence so it does not contain a double negative.**

5. I won't never watch another scary movie.

    _____

6. We don't never miss the school bus.

    _____

CHAPTER

6

Good and *Well*

● **Circle the letter of the word that correctly completes each sentence.**

1. Marie is a _____ storyteller.
   A. good
   B. well

2. Apples are _____ for your health.
   L. good
   M. well

3. Dave tap-dances very _____.
   H. good
   I. well

4. She read several _____ books over the summer.
   N. good
   O. well

5. We had a _____ time on our trip.
   C. good
   D. well

6. Benny swims _____.
   N. good
   O. well

7. I do not see _____ without my glasses.
   K. good
   L. well

8. Basketball is a _____ game.
   N. good
   O. well

● **Now write the circled letters, in order, on the numbered lines below. If your answers are correct, you will reveal the first initial and the last name of the first president to wear a beard in the White House.**

Answer: _____ . _____ _____ _____ _____ _____ _____ _____
             1   2   3   4   5   6   7   8

          Voyages in English 3

CHAPTER
6

Compound Sentences

● **Circle the conjunction that correctly completes each sentence.**

1. I bought tacos, (and   or) Clare bought burritos.

2. Brandon plays football, (or   but) his twin plays basketball.

3. Oscar can clean up his room, (or   but) he can take out the garbage.

4. Jane is always late, (or   but) Matt is often early.

5. The leader gave directions, (or   and) the scouts pitched the tents.

6. Maria takes tap lessons, (but   or) her real love is ballet.

7. The students can visit the monument, (but   or) they can explore the living history museum.

8. My sister loves clowns, (or   but) I don't think they're funny.

9. Our park has an ice rink, (and   but) we sometimes skate on it.

10. The guitar stood in the corner, (or   and) the flute was on the chair.

● **Make a compound sentence from each pair of sentences.**
 Use a conjunction.

11. I chose a sandwich. My friend had pizza.

 _____

12. Paula drew pictures. Her mother hung them on the refrigerator.

 _____

CHAPTER 6

To, *Too*, and *Two*

● **Cross out the incorrect sentence in each group. Then write it correctly on the line.**

1. Tonya bought two pencils.

2. Tonya bought erasers too.

3. Tonya spent too dollars.

_____

4. I went to a carnival this weekend.

5. I won to stuffed animals.

6. I won a basketball too.

_____

7. We drove to the party.

8. We brought gifts two.

9. We both ate two slices of cake.

_____

10. Are you taking swimming lessons too?

11. We can walk too the pool.

12. You have two more lessons this week.

_____

CHAPTER 6

Their and *There*

● **Write *correct* or *not correct* to identify the use of *their* and *there* in each sentence.**

1. Their uniforms are all muddy. _____

2. It is too expensive to eat their. _____

3. They washed there hands before dinner. _____

4. You can put your coat over there. _____

5. Let's sit there for our picnic. _____

6. We can visit them at their new home. _____

7. The children's backpacks are hanging their. _____

8. I can still see the spider up their. _____

9. He left his bat over there. _____

10. The chefs got sauce on there clothes. _____

● **Write two sentences that use *their* and *there* correctly.**

11. _____

_____

12. _____

_____

CHAPTER

6 Suffixes

● **Read the words in the word box. Think about the meaning of each suffix. Write each word in the blanks next to the matching definition.**

worthless	worker	pitcher	hopeless
thoughtless	spotless	cleaner	preacher

1. one who works   ___ ___ ___ ___ ___ ___
                                         4

2. without a spot   ___ ___ ___ ___ ___ ___ ___ ___
                              1

3. one who pitches   ___ ___ ___ ___ ___ ___ ___
                         8

4. without hope   ___ ___ ___ ___ ___ ___ ___ ___
                        7

5. without worth   ___ ___ ___ ___ ___ ___ ___ ___ ___
                      2

6. without thought   ___ ___ ___ ___ ___ ___ ___ ___ ___ ___
                        6

7. one who cleans   ___ ___ ___ ___ ___ ___ ___
                                   3

8. one who preaches   ___ ___ ___ ___ ___ ___ ___ ___
                          5

● **Now write the letters from the numbered blanks on the matching numbered lines below. If your answers are correct, you will reveal the answer to the riddle.**

What do you call a pig that knows karate?

Answer: A ___ ___ ___ ___ – ___ ___ ___ ___
           1   2   3   4   5   6   7   8

                 Voyages in English 3

CHAPTER 6

Coordinating Conjunctions

● **Circle the coordinating conjunction in each sentence. Underline the words or word groups that the conjunction joins.**

1. I can order pizza or pasta.

2. John is noisy but shy.

3. The kittens are sleeping on the bed and in the basket.

4. Will you use your fork or spoon to eat this thick soup?

5. This salsa is spicy but tasty.

6. Taylor does not like to cook or clean.

7. We walked through the forest and across the meadow.

● **You should have circled *or* in three sentences above. Find and circle the six words from these sentences that are joined by *or* in the word search below.**

```
B  O  R  T  P  I  Z  Z  A
J  C  L  E  A  N  T  Y  O
F  O  O  R  S  P  O  O  N
F  O  R  K  T  A  B  J  C
C  K  B  E  A  Z  Z  Y  M
```

CHAPTER
6

Self-Assessment

● Check *Always, Sometimes,* or *Never* to respond to each statement.

Writing	Always	Sometimes	Never
I can tell about the features of persuasive writing.			
I understand how to organize a persuasive article with a beginning, middle, and ending.			
I understand how to use an idea web to organize information.			
I can use conjunctions to make compound sentences.			
I can find the suffixes *-er* and *-less* and use them to understand the meaning of words.			

Grammar	Always	Sometimes	Never
I can find and use proper adjectives.			
I can find and use nouns used as adjectives.			
I can find and use adverbs.			
I can find and use adverbs that tell *when* or *how often.*			
I can find and use adverbs that tell *where.*			
I can find and use adverbs that tell *how.*			
I can find negative words and use them correctly.			
I can correctly use the words *good* and *well.*			
I can correctly use the words *to, too,* and *two.*			
I can correctly use the words *their* and *there.*			
I can find and use coordinating conjunctions.			

● **Write the most remarkable thing you learned in this chapter.**

_____

End Punctuation

● Write *tells*, *asks*, or *exclaims* to tell about each sentence. Then add
the correct punctuation at the end of the sentence.

1. How was your summer vacation   _____

2. My vacation was fantastic   _____

3. Kelly went camping in the mountains   _____

4. How exciting that is   _____

5. Were you excited   _____

6. It is cold on top of the mountain   _____

7. What a long hike we took   _____

8. We hiked ten miles   _____

9. Were you short of breath   _____

10. I rested along the way   _____

CHAPTER 7

Capital Letters

● **Add this editor's mark (≡) under the letters that should be capitalized.**

1. my teacher's favorite holiday is thanksgiving.

2. this is my friend sonya from england.

3. his brother kevin lives in montana.

4. the first day of school is in august.

5. my favorite day of the week is friday.

6. do you know who florence nightingale was?

● **Write three sentences. Use the name of a city, a street, and a holiday. Be sure to use capital letters correctly.**

7. _____

_____

8. _____

_____

9. _____

_____

CHAPTER 7

What Makes Good Realistic Fiction?

● **Write *yes* if the statement is true. Write *no* if the statement is not true. Rewrite each *no* statement to make it a *yes* statement.**

1. Realistic fiction tells about characters who seem real but are not. _____

   _____

2. Mysteries can be realistic fiction. _____

   _____

3. The characters in realistic fiction are always talking animals. _____

   _____

4. The problem in the story is called the setting. _____

   _____

5. Realistic fiction usually takes place in the future. _____

   _____

6. Characters do not have problems in realistic fiction. _____

   _____

7. The plot tells what happens in a story. _____

   _____

8. A plot has only a beginning and an ending. _____

   _____

CHAPTER 7

Abbreviations

● **Rewrite each word group. Use an abbreviation for each word in italics.**

1. *March* 5 to *April* 15   _____

2. the *gallon* of milk   _____

3. *Tuesday* and *Wednesday*   _____

4. 14 *North* Canal *Street*   _____

5. a *foot* of licorice   _____

6. one *pint* of juice   _____

7. *November* and *December*   _____

8. a *yard* of fabric   _____

● **Write a make-believe address. Use as many abbreviations as you can.**

_____

_____

_____

_____

CHAPTER 7

Personal Titles and Initials

- The people listed below are coming to your dinner party. Write a name card for each guest. Use periods and capital letters where they are needed. Use the text in parentheses to write the abbreviation of each person's title. The first one is done for you.

1.

    Gov. J. H. Jantsen

    (governor) j h jantsen

2.

    (mister) james e whittaker

3.

    (captain) a j prewitt

4.

    (mister) dave bunce

5.

    (an unmarried or a married woman)
    maria sanchez

6.

    (doctor) j m garcia

7.

    (an unmarried or a married woman)
    nancy moto

8.

    (a married woman)
    e chang

Characters

- **Use the story map to help you organize details for a realistic fiction story. Use your own story idea or choose one from the box. First, list details that describe the characters and the setting of your story. Next, list characters' actions that would be the main events of the story. Last, write a sentence that tells about the ending of the story. For an example of a story map, see page 137.**

> The main character is embarrassed to admit to friends that he or she cannot swim.
>
> The main character finds a bag of money under a bench in the park.
>
> The main character thinks the house next door is haunted.

Story Map

Characters:
Setting:
Main Events: 1. 2. 3. 4.
Ending:

Titles of Books and Poems

● **Read each title. Circle *correct* or *not correct* to tell if the title is written correctly. Rewrite each title that is not written or punctuated correctly.**

1. <u>James and the Giant Peach</u> (book) correct not correct

_____

2. <u>a matter of Taste</u> (poem) correct not correct

_____

3. "motorcycle Mouse" (book) correct not correct

_____

4. "A Visit from St. Nicholas" (poem) correct not correct

_____

5. <u>The Little Prince</u> (book) correct not correct

_____

6. "Diary of a Worm" (book) correct not correct

_____

7. <u>Daffodils</u> (poem) correct not correct

_____

8. <u>Going Home</u> (book) correct not correct

_____

Commas in a Series

CHAPTER 7

● Complete each sentence by writing a series of three nouns. Remember to use commas to separate the nouns. The first one is done for you.

1. Mrs. Olafson grows _____apples,_____ _____peaches,_____ and _____plums_____ in her orchard.

2. At the museum Janet saw _____ _____ and _____.

3. Animals that live in the woods include _____ _____ and _____.

4. I need to bring _____ _____ and _____ to school today.

5. Ahmed's favorite colors are _____ _____ and _____.

6. My little brother is scared of _____ _____ and _____.

7. I need to buy _____ _____ and _____ at the store.

8. Sheila is going to the concert with _____ _____ and _____.

9. The states we want to visit are _____ _____ and _____.

10. John sees _____ _____ and _____ at the beach.

CHAPTER 7 Dialog

● **Write a line of dialog for each dialog tag. Keep in mind who is speaking and how the person is speaking. Remember to include capital letters, quotation marks, and correct punctuation.**

1. The librarian whispered _____

2. Our gym teacher shouted _____

3. _____ groaned the rock climber.

4. _____ laughed Ben.

5. The patient sobbed _____

6. _____ raved the salesperson.

7. _____ yelled the firefighter.

8. The toddler whined _____

9. _____ suggested the teacher.

10. _____ pleaded the child.

● **Exchange your paper with a classmate. Compare the dialog you wrote for each dialog tag. Then write a line of dialog together for the dialog tag below.**

The excited fans shouted _____ .

CHAPTER 7

Commas in Direct Address

● **Read each pair of sentences. Circle the letter of the sentence that uses commas correctly.**

1. L. Please help me, fix this chair Becky.

    M. Please help me fix this chair, Becky.

2. E. Throw this rope, Tom, over the tree branch.

    F. Throw this rope Tom, over the tree branch.

3. H. Let's, take a vote class.

    G. Let's take a vote, class.

4. A. Crystal, I don't know the answer.

    B. Crystal I, don't know the answer.

5. B. Be careful, Ruben, with those scissors.

    C. Be careful Ruben, with those scissors.

6. I. To make the team, Deshawn, you must practice every day.

    H. To make the team, Deshawn you must practice every day.

7. T. Suzy, go to the store to buy some milk.

    U. Suzy go to the store, to buy some milk.

8. D. Maggie I, didn't know you could swim.

    E. Maggie, I didn't know you could swim.

● **Now write the circled letters, in order, on the numbered lines below. If your answers are correct, you will reveal the answer to the riddle.**

What do you get when you cross a mean bear with a computer?

Answer: A ____ ____ ____ ____ – ____ ____ ____ ____ !
           1   2   3   4   5   6   7   8

Commas in Compound Sentences

CHAPTER 7

● **Rewrite the paragraph. Combine shorter sentences to make at least three compound sentences. Remember to add a comma and the word _and_ or _but_.**

> Kevin waited patiently in the goal. He moved to the right side. He moved to the left side. His soccer team was winning by one goal. Kevin was doing a good job. His leg started to hurt. Suddenly, the ball was kicked above Kevin's head. He jumped up as high as the goal. He grabbed the ball. The referee blew the whistle. The game was over.

_____

_____

_____

_____

_____

_____

_____

_____

_____

_____

CHAPTER 7 Contractions

● **Circle the two words that correctly complete each sentence. Then write the two words as a contraction. The first one is done for you.**

1. have not   is not   will not

   I _____**won't**_____ forget my homework tomorrow.

2. will not   is not   does not

   She _____ cleaning her room right now.

3. was not   cannot   were not

   Fernando _____ go to the park today.

4. is not   will not   does not

   They _____ need to bring something.

5. will not   is not   have not

   Larry _____ read eight books by himself this month.

6. has not   will not   have not

   I _____ had so much fun by myself in a long time.

7. have not   has not   will not

   We _____ finished our spelling papers.

8. did not   are not   have not

   My friends said that they _____ been excited this week.

CHAPTER 7

Apostrophes

● **Circle the letter under *Possession* or *Contraction* to tell how the apostrophe is used in each italicized word.**

	Possession	Contraction
1. *Jim's* coat is warmer than mine.	K	P
2. She *won't* sing in public.	E	A
3. Jade *wasn't* able to see the show.	T	N
4. That is *Ashley's* necklace.	G	J
5. *Didn't* Mom leave a note?	I	A
6. *Sandy's* room is pink.	R	S
7. *I'll* take the garbage out tonight.	P	O
8. They *can't* take food into the theater.	J	O
9. There *isn't* room for one more person.	E	S

● **Now write the circled letters, in order, on the numbered lines below. If your answers are correct, you will reveal the name of leaping animals who travel in groups called mobs.**

Answer: ___ ___ ___ ___ ___ ___ ___ ___ ___
           1   2   3   4   5   6   7   8   9

Addresses

● **Rewrite two of the addresses on each envelope. Remember to use capital letters and commas where needed.**

mr. william cross
222 n. green st. apt. 2C
urbana il 61820

mrs. robyn nance
814 morningstar circle
belleville wa 50614

capt. nancy miller
50 e. cape rd.
salem nd 42443

dr. tracy peters
456 s. 22nd st. apt. 66
brunswick mo 05132

CHAPTER 7

Lines That Rhyme

● **Write two rhyming words for each word.**

1. sheep _____

2. mouse _____

3. whale _____

4. pig _____

● **Use a rhyming word for each underlined word to complete each couplet below.**

5. If you count a lot of <u>sheep</u>,

   Do you think you'll go to _____?

6. If you meet a cold little <u>mouse</u>,

   Give it a blanket from inside your _____.

7. Wouldn't it be funny to see a <u>whale</u>

   Carry a bag of letters and deliver the _____?

8. If you gave a shovel to a <u>pig</u>,

   Do you think it would help you _____?

CHAPTER
7

Direct Quotations

● **Read each riddle. Write the question and statements on the lines, using commas and quotation marks where needed.**

1. Tom: What does a rhinoceros do in a traffic jam?
   Ann: I don't know.
   Tom: He blows his horn!

   Tom asked _____

   _____ said Ann.

   Tom said _____

2. Kay: How can you tell if an elephant is under your bed?
   Lisa: I have no idea.
   Kay: Your nose is touching the ceiling.

   Kay asked _____

   _____ said Lisa.

   Kay said _____

3. Kelsey: What washes up on very small beaches?
   Dan: I give up.
   Kelsey: Microwaves!

   Kelsey asked _____

   Dan said _____

   _____ exclaimed Kelsey.

Name _____ Date _____

Self-Assessment

● Check *Always*, *Sometimes*, or *Never* to respond to each statement.

Writing	Always	Sometimes	Never
I can tell about the features of realistic fiction.			
I can describe the characters found in realistic fiction.			
I understand how to write and punctuate dialog.			
I can find and use contractions.			
I can name and write words that rhyme.			

Grammar	Always	Sometimes	Never
I can name and use end punctuation.			
I understand when to use capital letters.			
I can find and use common abbreviations.			
I can find and use abbreviations for personal titles and initials.			
I understand how to write the titles of books and poems.			
I understand how to use commas in a series.			
I understand how to use commas in direct address.			
I understand how to use commas in compound sentences.			
I understand how to use apostrophes with possessive nouns and contractions.			
I understand how to write addresses.			
I understand how to use quotation marks to set off a person's exact words.			

● **Write the most helpful thing you learned in this chapter.**

_____

CHAPTER 8

Subjects and Predicates

● **Diagram the sentences.**

1. Jane dances.

2. Grandpa rakes.

3. Jason runs.

4. Rabbits hop.

© Loyola Press

CHAPTER 8

Possessives

● **Diagram the sentences.**

1. Mom's ring sparkled.

2. Their wheels turn.

3. Kim's flowers grow.

4. Joellyn's brother sang.

CHAPTER 8

What Makes a Good Research Report?

- **Circle the letter of the answer that correctly completes each sentence.**

1. The purpose of a research report is to _____.
   a. give factual information
   b. convince the reader to believe you
   c. make the reader laugh

2. The introduction of a research report tells _____.
   a. what sources you used
   b. how the report ends
   c. what the topic is

3. The introduction should _____.
   a. narrow down the topic
   b. be written in steps
   c. grab the reader's attention

4. Details about the topic are found in the _____.
   a. introduction
   b. body
   c. conclusion

5. Details that are alike are grouped into _____.
   a. paragraphs
   b. topics
   c. graphics

6. A good conclusion _____.
   a. is found at the beginning of a research report
   b. contains a comment about the topic
   c. makes the reader laugh

7. Books, encyclopedia, and Internet Web sites are all examples of _____.
   a. details
   b. topics
   c. sources

8. You should always write facts _____.
   a. in the order you find them
   b. in your own words
   c. word for word from the source

CHAPTER

8

Adjectives

● **Diagram the sentences.**

1. Tired people sleep.

2. Green grass grows.

3. Happy dogs play.

4. Red leaves fall.

Adverbs

● **Diagram the sentences.**

1. Students whisper quietly.

2. People arrived early.

3. Waves crash loudly.

4. The team scored quickly.

CHAPTER 8

Facts and Notes

● **Think about a topic you are interested in researching for a report. Then fill in the K-W-L chart below. First, list facts you already know about your topic under *K*. Then write questions you have about your topic under *W*. Then look for the answers to your questions in sources from the library or on the Internet. Finally, write notes about your facts under *L*. For an example of a K-W-L chart, see page 138.**

K What I <u>K</u>no	W What I <u>W</u>ant to Kno	L What I <u>L</u>earned

CHAPTER

8

Adjectives as Complements

● **Diagram the sentences.**

1. Elephants are large.

2. Christy is athletic.

3. Pablo's hair is black.

4. The nurses were kind.

CHAPTER 8

Compound Subjects

● **Diagram the sentences.**

1. Louie and Sonny bark.

2. Cars and trains move quickly.

3. Doctors and nurses help.

4. Pitchers and catchers throw.

© Loyola Press

CHAPTER

8

Library Skills

- Complete each sentence about using the library with a word or words from the word box. You will not use all of the words.

fiction	nonfiction	call number	electronic catalogs	two
reference	title card	author card	subject card	three

1. Card catalogs have been replaced by _____ in many libraries today.

2. To find a _____ book, look for the last name of the author.

3. To find a _____ book, look up the subject of the book.

4. Dictionaries and encyclopedias are examples of _____ books.

5. A book's _____ is like an address because it tells where the book can be found.

6. If you only know the name of the book, find the _____.

7. If you only know who wrote the book, find the _____.

8. If you want to find information about a certain topic, find the

_____.

Compound Predicates

● **Diagram the sentences.**

1. Phil swims and splashes.

2. Toddlers wiggle and giggle.

3. The kitty stretched and yawned.

4. Cheetahs raced and rested.

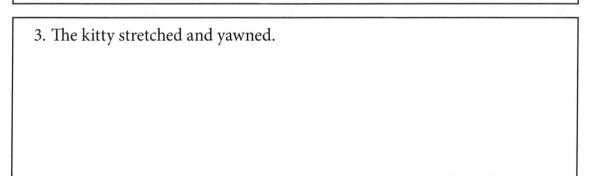

CHAPTER 8

Compound Complements

● **Diagram the sentences.**

1. Snowboarding was scary but exciting.

2. Basketballs are round and orange.

3. The salsa is hot and spicy.

4. The ride was fast but fun.

CHAPTER 8

Revising Sentences

● **Rewrite each sentence. Use a more exact word for the word in italics. Use a thesaurus if you need help.**

1. The skier *moved* around the trees on the run.

_____

2. The test we just took was *hard*.

_____

3. Everyone was afraid to knock on the door of the *old* house.

_____

4. We couldn't go outside because of the *bad* weather.

_____

5. The injured athlete *walked* to the locker room.

_____

● **Combine each set of sentences to create one sentence.**

6. Sofia is kind. She is also generous.

_____

7. This salsa is spicy. It is delicious.

_____

8. We can go snorkeling. We can take a harbor cruise too.

_____

Compound Sentences

● **Diagram the sentences.**

1. Kyle slept, and Dad drove.

2. The team scored, and the fans cheered.

3. Balls bounced, and whistles blew.

4. Some apples are sweet, and some apples are tart.

Diagramming Practice

● **Diagram the sentences.**

1. Cows wander.

2. Jana speaks quietly.

3. The trees are tall.

4. The furniture is old.

Homophones

- **Circle the homophone in parentheses that correctly completes each sentence.**

1. I will (right   write) a letter to my grandmother.

2. The (knight   night) rode in on a black stallion.

3. Cherise wants to (be   bee) a nurse.

4. Dad (ate   eight) the last slice of pizza.

5. (Your   You're) going to be late if you don't hurry.

6. The (plane   plain) leaves at one o'clock.

7. That boy is our teacher's (sun   son).

8. The train traveled (threw   through) the tunnel.

9. Amir's party starts in one (our   hour).

10. Would you like to (meat   meet) my parents?

- **Write two sentences with the homophones *here* and *hear*.**

11. _____

_____

12. _____

_____

CHAPTER 8

More Diagramming Practice

● **Diagram the sentences.**

1. Diamonds and stars twinkle.

2. The acrobats ran and tumbled.

3. The cheerleaders are loud and spirited.

4. The fruit was tasty, but the rolls were delicious.

CHAPTER 8 Self-Assessment

● Check *Always*, *Sometimes*, or *Never* to respond to each statement.

Writing	Always	Sometimes	Never
I can tell about the features of a research report.			
I understand how to find facts and take notes for a research report.			
I can use a library to find different types of resources.			
I understand how to revise sentences with exact words and combined sentences.			
I can name homophones and use them correctly.			

Grammar	Always	Sometimes	Never
I can diagram subjects and predicates in sentences.			
I can diagram sentences with possessive nouns.			
I can diagram sentences with adjectives.			
I can diagram sentences with adverbs.			
I can diagram sentences with adjectives used as complements.			
I can diagram sentences with compound subjects.			
I can diagram sentences with compound predicates.			
I can diagram sentences with compound complements.			
I can diagram compound sentences.			

● **Why do you think diagramming sentences is useful?**

_____

Story Map

Characters: me, my mom, my little brother

Setting: a pumpkin patch at a farm

Main Events:
1. rode into patch on a wagon pulled by a tractor
2. picked our pumpkins
3. tractor driver forgot us
4. walked 1 mile back to farm

Ending: got free pumpkins and a homemade dinner from the farmer's wife

Sequence Chart

Topic: How to Braid

1. Divide hair into three sections.

2. Cross the right section over the middle. Pull tight.

3. Cross the left section over the middle. Pull tight.

4. Keep overlapping right to left until you get to the end of the hair.

5. Fasten with a hair band.

Conclusion: You can make one big braid or many small braids, depending on how many sections of hair you braid.

K-W-L Chart

What I Know	What I Want to Know	What I Learned
Jackie Robinson was the first African-American baseball player in the major leagues.	1. When did he play in his first game? 2. Who signed him? 3. Was he accepted at first?	1. April 15, 1947 2. Branch Rickey, president of the Brooklyn Dodgers 3. No. He got hate mail and some pitchers tried to hit him with the ball, but he was finally accepted. 4. He helped fight for civil rights his whole adult life.

Fact-and-Opinion Chart

Fact

In 1997 scientists discovered fossilized dinosaur eggs in Argentina.

The eggs were from a titanosaur.

The eggs measured 18 inches long.

Opinion

Dinosaurs were cool.

Someday scientists will know everything about dinosaurs.

Studying dinosaurs is exciting.